★BRUCE★SPRINGSTEEN★

JAMES R. ROTHAUS

CREATIVE EDUCATION

Copyright ©1986 by Creative Education, Inc. International copyrights reserved in all countries. No part of this book may be reproduced in any form without written permission from the publisher.
Printed in the United States.

Library of Congress Cataloging-in-Publication Data

Rothaus, James.
  Bruce Springsteen.

  Summary: A biography of a rock musician whose extra-ordinarily successful career is marked by demonstrations of caring about everyday people.

  1. Springsteen, Bruce—Juvenile literature. 2. Rock musicians—United States—Biography—Juvenile literature. [1. Springsteen, Bruce. 2. Musicians] I. Title.
ML3930.S72R7 1986   784.5'4'00924 [B] [92]   86-23966
ISBN 0-88682-099-5

Photographic Credits
  Ray Amati: Cover, 4, 12, 14, 19, 23, 29
  FPG International, Mark Harlan: 9, 32
  Wide World Photo: 3

"I was prepared to be disappointed in Bruce Springsteen," wrote Seattle rock critic Mitchell Carter back in 1978.

"Before the Springsteen concert at Paramount Northwest I stood outside in the rain and eavesdropped on small groups of his loyal fans. Unlike me, some had seen Springsteen up-close in previous concerts. They spoke of their hero as if he were a genius, the Einstein of music, the Beethoven of rock and roll.

"No one, not even Springsteen, can be *that* good," I thought to myself. "But I was wrong, and they were right.

"Bruce Springsteen's music is magical. His energy and stage presence are heroic. His raw honesty moved me to laughter and to tears. By the end of the show I found myself standing in the aisle, swaying to the music, hypnotized by the man and his message.

"If Springsteen can do this now," I thought, "what will he be doing ten years from now?"

THE BOSS MOVES ON

A decade later, the man they call "The Boss" is still roaming the world as the most acclaimed figure in American rock.

Year after year, his special music and lyrics have

Bruce was born in Freehold, New Jersey, to Adele and Douglas Springsteen on September 23, 1949. He and his two younger sisters — Virginia and Pamela — had to share the same small bedroom in the early days, as their father and mother struggled to make ends meet.

built new bridges between the old and the young.

His tours have made countless friends for America in many foreign countries around the world.

Here at home, his endless string of benefit concerts and other charitable activities have raised more than money for the homeless and disadvantaged. They have healed the hearts of Vietnam veterans, breathed new hope into the lives of American farmers, and restored a sense of dignity to tens of thousands of laid-off workers.

Simply put, Springsteen has demonstrated that he cares — *truly cares* — about everyday people, and that he has his own special ways of showing it.

When his album *The River* was ready to debut in June 1980 as a two-record set, Bruce waged a quiet battle with the big shots at Columbia records. In his typical soft-serious way, he insisted they lower the price of the album because, "Hey, I know what it's like to be a teenager. You love music, but you're broke. Now, what? Go without? Steal it?"

Enough said. Columbia granted the unusual request. The album was released to rave reviews, and Springsteen took his E Street Band on an eleven-month tour that rocked the nation and much of Western Europe.

The River tour took a toll on Bruce. As always, he insisted on giving his total energy to every crowd at every stop in every city along the way. An all-out, three-hour marathon performance with several curtain calls was the rule.

After shows, in the early morning hours, in his hotel lobby, in coffee shops, parking lots or elevators, Springsteen somehow made time for autographs, snapshots or rap sessions with his fans.

"If they care enough to wait around for me," he would tell reporters, "I always gotta find a way to be there for them, too. I'm one of them, and they are what the music is all about."

At one point, the tour was temporarily halted. The news went out that Springsteen was suffering from exhaustion. "Slow down, Bruce," cautioned E Street guitarist Steve Van Zandt, his close friend and stage partner.

Instead, Springsteen added even more stops to the summer portion of the tour, including an August 20 benefit concert in Los Angeles that raised $100,000 for the Vietnam Veterans of America.

"Lots of celebrities talk about the plight of the Vietnam vet," said the organization's vice-president, Michael Harbert. "Springsteen *does* something about it. There isn't a phony bone in his body. The man is for real."

By 1982, the year his fabled *Nebraska* folk album was released, Springsteen's reputation for giving of himself had already spread far and wide.

If you followed the newspapers over the next cou-

ple years, Bruce and friends seemed to be everywhere all at once. No, they weren't seeking publicity, but they got it.

One news story shows them quietly bolstering the spirits of unemployed steel workers. Another shows them rallying donations for a small inner-city food bank. Yet another shows them saluting the social workers at a Midwest halfway house for recovering addicts. It was a sign of things to come.

Meanwhile, the stark, melancholy songs in *Nebraska* went out across the airways.

Singing solo on *Nebraska*, Bruce simply and clearly reflects the feelings experienced by lonely, frustrated people during hard times. The album was recorded on Springsteen's four-track, portable home cassette recorder. It was his no-frills way of calling attention to everyday people all around us who, for one reason or another, feel abandoned and friendless. He asks all of us to reach down inside ourselves to find big and little ways to reach out to our neighbors.

"I think Nebraska finally showed the world the size of this man's heart," said Clarence 'Big Man' Clemons, the band's burly saxophonist. "I know the Boss (Springsteen) for what he is, and I've never known another one quite like him.

"As an artist, Bruce stands alone. As a human being, he's all heart. Feeling, caring and giving is what he's all about. People sense this about him. In a world filled with hype and jive, we're attracted to something honest and real. That's Springsteen, and that's his music too."

BORN IN THE USA

By now everyone knows the story of the album that followed *Nebraska*. All during 1983, there had been rumors about "something big" in the works. Springsteen was back in the studio with the E Street Band. Or, was he? The year came and went, and still no album.

Meanwhile, a strange collection of leather-clad heavy metal bands, pink-haired punkers and sequined country-western groups took over the charts.

"Where are you, Bruce?" wondered mainstream rock fans throughout America. The winter of 1984 dragged into spring, and still no Springsteen.

Then it happened. In a dizzying series of media events, Bruce and the E Street Band made their presence felt in a big way.

On April 15, 1984, the rock world was stunned by the news that Bruce's longtime sidekick, Steve Van Zandt, was leaving the band to do his own thing. That was the bad news.

The good news came on May 4 when Springsteen's long-awaited new single—*Dancing In The Dark Pink Cadillac*—debuted across the country.

"*Dancing In The Dark* is an unexpectedly upbeat song for Springsteen," wrote a delighted Elianne Halbersberg in her popular book, *The Boss*. "It has all the makings of a chart hit—uplifting tempo, sing-along harmonies, a catchy chorus, lots of backbeat. But those comtemporary ingredients are just surface characteristics.

"Lyrically," explained Halbersberg, "*Dancing In The Dark* is still one-hundred percent Springsteen—the frustrated person looking for something different, dissatisfied with himself, in need of a change of action.

"Springsteen has again captured the agitation and futility that so many of us feel; our inner conflicts, the lack of confidence, the urge to make something happen, combined with the uncertainty of exactly what it is we are looking for."

Two weeks later, *Rolling Stone* magazine announced that the electrifying Nils Lofgren had been recruited to take Steve Van Zandt's place on guitar.

Wait, there's more. Bruce also whisked unknown vocalist Patti Scialfa into the E Street lineup after he heard her sing in a night club back in Asbury Park, his stomping grounds.

On June 5, *Born in the U.S.A.* was released to radio stations around the country. Immediately, the request lines lit up. The Boss was back, and the stage was set for the rock tour of the decade.

THE BOSS IS BACK

The evening of June 29, 1984, brought moonlight, warm summer winds and an historic event to the fans who jammed the streets leading to the Civic Center in St. Paul, Minnesota. Springsteen had chosen this city as the launch point for the big road trip.

When Bruce and the E Street Band took the stage that night, a sweet-sounding roar welled up from the crowd, swept through the arena, and washed over the band.

The security guards stood in wonder. There on the stage was the greatest rock legend in the land. The guards had expected the same old obscenities, fights and vandalism that had marred the heavy metal concerts at that arena. Instead, this crowd was friendly, loving and joyful.

Instead of leather, spikes and fancy jewelry, Springsteen was dressed plainly and comfortably in faded jeans, cotton shirt and his favorite work boots. His clear eyes, sparkling smile and lean muscular body evidenced his commitment to clean living: Six miles of daily jogging; no drugs, alcohol, cigarettes or junk food.

"St. Paul Crowns You King!" read one of the banners unfurled along the balcony. "Tell Us How It Is!" read another. And so he did.

That night, as he would on every other night

Some of his old classmates recall that Bruce was a smart, intense kid who remained physically small and kind of homely through high school. He loved baseball and football, but didn't excel at either. There were no girls in his life, and he had very few friends.

Because of his long hair and patched jeans, Bruce was considered to be a bit of a rebel by his teachers, but he wasn't a troublemaker. He was simply a loner who stuck to himself and his love for music.

throughout the 14-month tour, Bruce warmed and inspired the crowd with a thoughtful blend of the *Nebraska* and *Born in the U.S.A.* material, occasionally pulling unexpected cuts from previous albums, or one of his many songs made famous by other artists.

With Springsteen, each performance is fresh and different in many ways, but the same in one. There's never a dull moment, never a possiblity that Bruce himself will stagger out on the stage drunk or loaded, never a hint that he is giving anything less than his best in every way.

While other rock stars rely on bodyguards to protect them from being mobbed, Bruce wanders freely into the crowd, confident that he is one with his fans. No other performer today receives such love and respect.

Elianne Halbersberg explains: "Springsteen and Band don't perform for the audience; they perform with them.

"When Springsteen tells one of his stories, he's telling it to 20,000 of his closest friends.

"When he extends the microphone to the audience, the entire crowd sings ... his energy level never subsides by even one degree. The constant drive—just pure rock and roll the way it was meant to be and, thanks to Springsteen, the way it is again—leaves the audience physically exhausted but emotionally gratified for days after the concert.

"Even the strictest security guards have been known to clap their hands and join in on the chorus!"

In all, more than four million people paid to see Springsteen on tour in *Born in the U.S.A.* It is difficult to say how many others were turned away.

More than 15,000 tickets were sold in a single one-hour period for his New York concert. One desperate fan in New Jersey placed an unusual ad in the classified section, alongside dozens of other pleas for Springsteen tickets: "Will trade my $450 stereo for two tickets to The Boss."

The album went platinum. Halfway through the tour it had already sold five million copies—almost twice his previous high with the earlier *Born to Run* album—and there was no end in sight.

As for Bruce, he took it all in stride. When a Connecticut reporter asked him how it felt to be rich, famous, idolized by millions and number one on the charts, Bruce looked up slowly and winced. Just the thought of being characterized as a big-deal celebrity obviously caused him pain.

"I gotta tell you that the money and the rest of it don't mean much to me," Bruce patiently explained. "If you're in it for that, you don't belong on the stage, you don't belong in rock and roll.

"The whole idea is to reach people with the

music, not line your own pockets or get caught in the trap of believing all the great things people say about you.

"Rock and roll is my reason to live, so I've gotta be true to it and true to myself. Right now, thousands of people come to see us play, but I'd still be playing even if I was in a small club in front of 10 or 20 people."

STRAIGHT FROM THE HEART

What does it mean to be "true" to rock and roll? It's the kind of question that would probably make legions of parents very uncomfortable.

For many years, the term "rock music" was associated with sneering rebels, irresponsible greasers, fast cars and endless parties.

In the 1950's, horrified parents shuddered at the sight of Jerry Lee Lewis banging on the piano keyboard with his feet.

They switched off the television when Elvis Presley brought his tight-fitting clothes, drooping eyelids and gyrating hips to the nationally televised Ed Sullivan Show.

They puzzled over the shrill-sounding "Oooweee, Baby" lyrics of early black rock stars such as Little Richard and soul singer James Brown.

Later, in the Sixties and Seventies, rock was marked by the searing tribal energy of Eric Burdon and The Animals, the Rolling Stones, Gary "U.S." Bonds, the various Motown groups and—well, not one of them earned the PTA seal of approval. Eventually, rock and roll became associated with drugs, defiance, wildness, sex and little else.

What does it mean, then, when someone like Bruce Springsteen says that he intends to be "true" to rock and roll?

"It means singin' from the heart about things that count," explains Springsteen, "but you can't just sing it, you've gotta be it. Too many people in this business have said one thing, and then went off and lived somethin' else. I'm not passin' judgment on anyone, I'm just sayin' that I don't want to fall into the same old traps."

Those closest to Bruce believe he may be referring to the exhilarating rise and depressing decline of Elvis Presley and some of the other legends of rock's earlier years.

It was Elvis' historic appearance on the Ed Sullivan Show in 1957 that first gave Springsteen the idea to get a guitar.

Like Elvis, Bruce grew up in a rundown working-class neighborhood. Though Elvis' family lived in the deep south and Bruce's lived in little Freehold, New Jersey near the Eastern Seaboard, the situation was equally grim and depressing.

Here, as in hundreds of similar blue-collar pockets throughout America, most people had given up hope of ever enjoying the nice things promised by the American Dream—the basic things like a good, steady job, a nice home of your own and a sense of confidence in the future.

"Where I come from, you're born, go to school, get a job in a factory and settle down in a house like the one on either side of you," explains Bruce. "One day you wake up and realize you got no hope. You're just puttin' in time like everyone else.

"Where's the meaning in your life? You feel bad enough to fight, scream, drink or cry. You want someone—anyone—to know what you're feelin' inside, how frustrated and lost you are, how sad and angry you're gettin'. Rock and roll speaks to you; it connects you to someone or something that's just like what's in your heart."

Springsteen was only nine-years-old the night he saw Elvis on TV, but the experience sparked a sense of excitement in him that would eventually fire his entire life with purpose. In his book, *Born To Run, The Bruce Springsteen Story*, author Dave Marsh recounts Bruce's feelings:

"'Man, when I was nine, I couldn't imagine anyone not wanting to be Elvis Presley,' Springsteen remembered years later.

"In 1963, even before the advent of the Beatles, lightning struck. 'I was dead until I was thirteen,'

Bruce says, and he means it. 'I didn't have any way of getting my feelings out . . . so I bought a guitar.' With it came an identity.

"This guitar came from a pawnshop, for $18. 'It was one of the most beautiful sights I'd ever seen in my life. It was a magic scene. There it is: The Guitar. It was real and it stood for something: Now you're real. I had found a way to do everything I wanted to do.'

"His cousin Frankie taught him his first few chords. The thrill was immediate. Since the day he began, Springsteen says, 'Rock and roll has been everything to me. The first day I can remember looking in a mirror and being able to stand what I was seeing was the day I had a guitar in my hand.'"

If the guitar brought meaning to Springsteen's life, it also brought a growing sense of sadness and responsibility.

The sadness, of course, came as Bruce watched those gifted rock stars rise with such promise, only to self-destruct. Instant wealth, high living, phony people and drugs—all took their toll on Bruce's idols. Even Elvis, whose early career had seemed so brilliant and durable, eventually died tragically amid rumors of drug abuse.

"In the Greensboro Coliseum in 1985, Springsteen was still talking about Elvis," writes Robert Hilburn in *Springsteen*.

Bruce was only fifteen when he landed a spot as a guitar player with the Castiles, a local group that played at high school dances or small town functions in Freehold.

At first, he was the no-name guitarist in the background, but eventually his confidence grew and he tried a few vocals. "I surprised myself," he recalls. "It began to dawn on me that I knew as much as some of the older guys in the band. Maybe more. I thought, Hmmmm, what can you really do?"

"Only this time his tone was different. Early in the concert, he told about driving by Graceland (Presley's mansion) in 1976. Springsteen laughed as he recalled how he climbed the wall and raced to Elvis' front door, hoping to get a chance to meet him. He was caught and turned away by the guards with no sight of Elvis.

"He then described his feelings when he learned that Elvis died. 'It was hard to understand how somebody whose music took away so many people's loneliness could have ended up as lonely as he did.' Springsteen began singing, *Bye, Bye Johnny*, a song he wrote shortly after Presley's death. It's a mournful tune that ends, 'You didn't have to die, you didn't have to die.'"

A NEW AMERICAN SYMBOL

Elvis was known as the king of rock and roll, and Springsteen now finds himself in the position of inheriting the throne. He didn't plan it this way, it just happened. Somehow, millions of fans across the nation are willing to entrust more faith in him, his message and his music than they are willing to entrust in their top politicians.

Running for reelection to the Presidency in 1984, Ronald Reagan singled Bruce out in a speech delivered to a crowd in Hammonton, N.J.

"America's future," said the President, "rests

in a thousand dreams inside your hearts. It rests in the message of hope in songs of a man so many young Americans admire—New Jersey's own Bruce Springsteen."

And so, a growing sense of responsibility has fallen on the shoulders of the newly-crowned king of rock and roll. "The bigger you get, the more responsibility you have," Bruce has said. "So you have got to keep constant vigilance. You got to keep your strength up because if you lose it, then you're just another jerk who had his picture on the cover."

Chet Flippo, a writer for *People* magazine, explained that Bruce is "taking over the mike as spokesman for people who've been speechless all too long: Vietnam vets and blue collar workers who were just scraping by and wondering what had happened to their American dream, ordinary people who loved their rock 'n' roll and their nation and weren't quite sure where they fit in anymore, or if they fit in at all."

Where does Bruce himself fit in? The kids who live in his native New Jersey have a pet saying that probably answers that question in a few words. "You gotta walk the talk," they like to say. Translation: Talk is cheap. The true measure of a person's life lies in how that person actually follows through on what he says.

That's the magic in Bruce Springsteen. Remove

the guitar, the bright lights, the blaring sound system and the roaring crowds, and you still have something wonderful, real and durable.

You have a young man who is convinced that things—money or material possessions—do not make a good world; people do. You have a man who writes songs about honesty, compassion, trust and integrity—the stuff that lasts long after all the glitter and tinsel around us has rusted away. Most of all, you have someone who invites our trust because "he walks the talk." He takes action on the things in which he believes.

In May of 1986, the Entertainment section of a large West Coast newspaper was peppered with several lengthy stories about the latest groups to hit the rock scene. One photo showed a tall, thin male guitarist dressed in a black cape and what appeared to be lace women's underwear. Another photo showed four laughing members of a British heavy metal band being arrested by Los Angeles police for allegedly wrecking a hotel room.

At the bottom of the same page of the same newspaper was a brief column marked "Postscripts." There, in small type and with no headline, was the following item:

"Bruce Springsteen and a group of New Jersey musicians will make a video of "We've Got The Love" at a community food bank in Newark, N.J.,

Every fan has his or her favorite Springsteen story. Here's a typical one from writer Laura Fissinger: "Once, Bruce rented a car and drove off for a movie by himself. Outside the theater a young fan recognized him and asked Bruce to sit with him and his sister during the film. Bruce did. Afterward, the boy asked Bruce to come home and meet his parents. Bruce did that too!

"Later Bruce happily told a reporter that the incident was an example of the wonderful things his job lets him do. Through his music he is able to enter the lives of many different people."

tomorrow. Proceeds from New Jersey sales of the single, which Arista Records is releasing to world distribution next month, will go to the food bank. Proceeds from sales elsewhere will go to local food programs and related charities."

Thank you, Bruce Springsteen.